HANUKKAH

by
Cathy Goldberg Fishman

illustrations by
Mary O'Keefe Young

Carolrhoda Books, Inc./Minneapolis

For the patient ears of Laurie, Sherri, Elise, and Nancy — C. G. F.

For my loved ones: Peree, Brendan, Myles, Dana, and Maggie — M. O'K. Y

Special thanks to Rabbi Jordan Parr for his help with the preparation of this book.

Publisher's Note: The land in which the Hanukkah story takes place is sometimes referred to as Judah but is more commonly known as Judea. We have chosen to use the more common name for the region.

This book is available in two editions:
Library binding by Carolrhoda Books, Inc., a division of Lerner Publishing Group
Soft cover by First Avenue Editions, an imprint of Lerner Publishing Group
241 First Avenue North
Minneapolis, MN 55401 U.S.A.

Website address: www.lernerbooks.com

Library of Congress Cataloging-in-Publication Data

Fishman, Cathy Goldberg.
    Hanukkah / by Cathy Goldberg Fishman ; illustrations by Mary O'Keefe Young.
       p.   cm. — (On my own holidays)
    Summary: Introduces the Jewish Festival of Lights, or Hanukkah, relating the story behind the holiday and how it is celebrated.
    ISBN: 1–57505–195–8 (lib. bdg. : alk. paper)
    1. Hanukkah—Juvenile literature. [1. Hanukkah. 2. Holidays.] I. Young, Mary O'Keefe, ill. II. Title. III. Series.
BM695.H3 F58 2004
296.4'35—dc21   2002006814

Manufactured in the United States of America
1 2 3 4 5 6 – JR – 09 08 07 06 05 04

HANUKKAH

For eight nights each winter,
Jews all over the world celebrate
a holiday filled with light.
The holiday is called Hanukkah.
Sometimes Hanukkah is also called
the Festival of Lights.

Every Hanukkah,
Jews remember an amazing story.
They remember events that happened more
than two thousand years ago.
The story begins in Judea,
in the ancient land of Israel.

The Jewish people had lived in Judea
for hundreds of years.
But they had not ruled over their land
for many years.

The Jews were not soldiers or kings.

They were farmers and shepherds.

They were teachers and merchants.

A group of people called

the Syrian Greeks ruled over Judea.

The Syrian Greeks and the Jews

followed different religions.

The Syrian Greeks believed in many gods.

The Jews believed in only one God.

But the Syrian Greeks and the Jews

lived together in peace.

The most holy place for the Jews
was in the city of Jerusalem.
High on a hill stood their Temple.

Jews traveled from distant towns
just to visit the Temple.
They came there to celebrate their holidays.

Inside the Temple was a beautiful
oil lamp called a menorah.
It had seven places that burned
special oil.

The menorah was made of gold.

It burned day and night.

The bright light reminded

the Jewish people of their God.

Everything changed for the Jews
when a cruel new ruler
gained power in Judea.
His name was Antiochus the Fourth.

Antiochus saw how different the Jews
were from the Syrian Greeks.
He disliked the different ways
of the Jews.
He wanted them to follow the Greek
religion and pray to Greek gods.

Some Jews listened to Antiochus.

But most shut their ears to him.

Antiochus grew angry.

He made a new law.

The law said that Jews could not

pray to their God.

They could not celebrate their holidays.

If they did these things,

they would be arrested and killed.

This new law did not change the Jews.

Most of them still did not obey Antiochus.

Antiochus grew angrier and angrier.

He ordered his soldiers to break into
the Jewish Temple.

The soldiers put statues of Greek gods inside.

They broke open the pots of special oil.

They knocked over
the beautiful gold menorah.

And the light of the Temple went out.

Many Jews ran away from Jerusalem.
They hoped to keep their religion
in secret.
But Antiochus sent soldiers after them.
A Jewish leader named Mattathias
would not give in to Antiochus.

Mattathias lived in a small town
outside of Jerusalem.
He and his five sons decided
to fight Antiochus.
They would become soldiers
for the Jewish people.

Other Jewish farmers joined Mattathias
in his fight.
But Mattathias was an old man.
He soon died.
His son Judah became the new leader.
People called him Judah Maccabee.
Maccabee means hammer in Hebrew,
the language of the Jews.
Judah's army was called the Maccabees,
the hammers.

The Maccabees were strong.

But Antiochus's army was stronger.

Antiochus had many soldiers and horses.

His soldiers had powerful weapons.

They even had elephants

that had been taught to fight.

The Maccabees were a small group
of farmers.
They did not have horses or elephants.
Their only weapons were farming tools.
But they were not afraid.
And they would not give up.

The Jewish people fought
for three long years.
They would not quit.
Their army was always smaller
than the army of Antiochus.
But something amazing happened.

Judah Maccabee and his small army
beat Antiochus's powerful army.
They won the battle to be free.
It was a miracle!
The Jews believed that their God had
helped them win their war for freedom.

Jewish men and women marched
right into Jerusalem.
They went straight to the Temple.
The Temple was in ruins.
Grass was growing inside.
The statues of Greek gods were still there.
Shattered pots of oil lay on the ground.

The Jews pulled out the grass.

They took out the statues.

They cleaned up the Temple.

Then they rededicated
the Temple to God.

They made the Temple
holy again for God.

Judah Maccabee lit the menorah
and brought back the light.
He called for that day to be a new holiday.
He named the holiday Hanukkah,
the Hebrew word for dedication.
He commanded the Jewish people
to celebrate Hanukkah every year.

Some people say another miracle
happened on that first Hanukkah.
They say that Judah Maccabee could find
only a single pot of pure oil for the menorah.
It was just enough oil to burn for one day.
But the oil burned for eight days.
That small bit of oil burned long enough
for the Jews to find more oil.

Jewish people still celebrate Hanukkah
every year.
They remember the miracles
and the fight for freedom.
Sometimes Hanukkah comes at the end
of November.
Sometimes it comes in December.
But it always begins on the same day
of the Hebrew calendar,
the calendar of the Jews.
It begins on the 25th day
of the Hebrew month of Kislev.
That day is the same day that Judah
Maccabee lit the menorah in the Temple.
For eight days and nights,
Jewish families light their own menorahs.

They light them in their homes and in
their synagogues, their places of worship.
They light the candles at night
when the first stars appear.

The Hanukkah menorah is called
a hanukkiah.

It has places for nine candles.

There is one place for each night
of Hanukkah.

And there is one place for a candle
called the shamash.

Shamash means helper in Hebrew.

The shamash is used
to light all the other candles.

On the first night, a candle is put in
the farthest right place of the hanukkiah.

Someone lights the shamash and uses it
to light the first night's candle.

Everyone says Hanukkah prayers
as the candles are lit.

Then the shamash goes back in its place.

The two candles burn all the way down.

On each night of Hanukkah,

more candles go in the hanukkiah.

They are put in from right to left.

And they are lit from left to right

with the shamash candle.

The light of the candles

glows brighter and brighter.

Some families have one hanukkiah.

They light it together.

Some families have a hanukkiah for each
person to light.

Many families place a hanukkiah
in a window.

They share the miracles of Hanukkah
with the world outside.

Lighting candles is not the only way
to remember the story of Hanukkah.
There are special foods to eat, too.
One food is called latkes.
Latkes are potato pancakes fried in oil.

Another Hanukkah treat
is called sufganiyot.
Sufganiyot are jelly donuts fried in oil.
The oil of the latkes and sufganiyot reminds
people of the Hanukkah story.
It reminds them of the oil that burned
for eight days in the Temple.

Jewish children remember Hanukkah
with a favorite holiday game.
The game is called dreidel.
A dreidel is a small spinning top
with four sides.

Each of the sides has a Hebrew letter on it.
The letters are the first letters of each
word in a Hebrew sentence.
The sentence means "A great miracle
happened there."
It reminds the children of the Maccabees
and their fight for freedom long ago.
On Hanukkah, Jewish children take turns
spinning the dreidel.

Hanukkah is also a time for family
and friends.
Some Jews decorate their homes
and have a party.

Everyone eats latkes and sufganiyot.

They sing songs.

They give each other presents.

They dance and read stories together.

But, mostly, Hanukkah is a time

for the Jewish people to remember.

They remember the story

of the Maccabees.

They remember the light of the miracles.

And they remember how good

it is to be free.

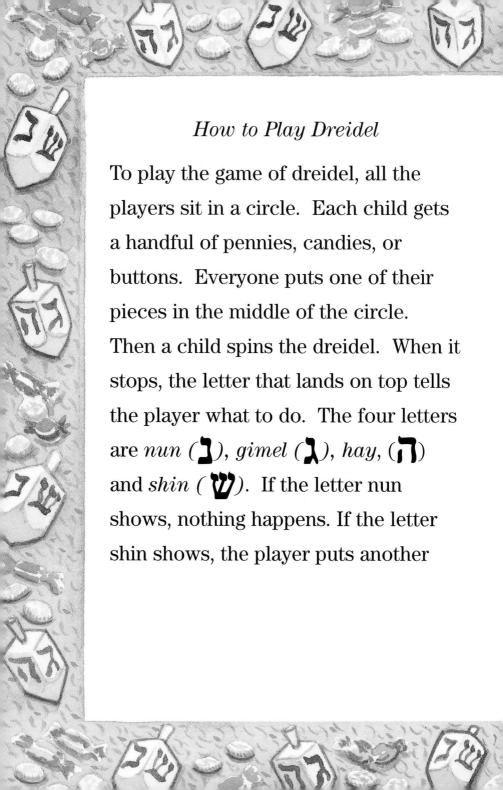

How to Play Dreidel

To play the game of dreidel, all the
players sit in a circle. Each child gets
a handful of pennies, candies, or
buttons. Everyone puts one of their
pieces in the middle of the circle.
Then a child spins the dreidel. When it
stops, the letter that lands on top tells
the player what to do. The four letters
are *nun* (נ), *gimel* (ג), *hay,* (ה)
and *shin* (ש). If the letter nun
shows, nothing happens. If the letter
shin shows, the player puts another

piece in the middle. If the letter hay shows, the player gets half of what is in the middle. If the letter gimel shows, the player gets everything in the middle. Then, everyone puts another piece in the middle to fill it up again. It is the next player's turn. The person with the most pieces at the end of the game is the winner.

New Words

Antiochus (an-tee-AH-kuhs): ruler of Judea during the time of the Maccabees

Dreidel (DRAY-duhl): a spinning top with four sides, and part of a Hanukkah game

Hanukkah (CHAH-noo-kah): a Jewish celebration meaning "dedication"

Hanukkiah (chah-noo-kee-YAH): a candleholder with nine branches used during Hanukkah

Latkes (LAHT-kuhz): potato pancakes fried in oil

Maccabee (MAC-uh-bee): the name for Judah and his army; Maccabee means "hammer" in Hebrew.

Mattathias (mat-uh-THY-us): leader of the fight against Antiochus

Menorah (meh-NOHR-uh): an oil lamp with seven branches

Shamash (SHAH-mahsh): the helper candle used to light other candles in a hanukkiah

Sufganiyot (SOOF-gah-nee-yoht): jelly donuts fried in oil

Note on pronunciation: In Hebrew, the *ch* denotes a throaty *H* sound.